Also available in Magnet:

The Papier Mâché Book *by Claudine Loiselot-Nicostrate*
Make Up For Fun *by Patric Parmentier / Quat'Bulles*
Fingerplay *by Lafeuille / Patrice Veres*

First published in Great Britain in 1988
as a Magnet paperback by Methuen Children's Books Ltd
11 New Fetter Lane, London EC4P 4EE
Copyright © 1986 Dessain et Tolra, Paris
English text by Juliet Peters
Copyright © 1988 by Methuen Children's Books

Printed in Italy by Tipolitografia G. Canale & C. S.p.A. - Turin
ISBN 0 416 08542 3

Face Painting

Jean-Paul Alègre
and the Theatre du Fil d'Ariane

English text by Juliet Peters

A Magnet Book

Contents

Preface

At almost any fair, fête or carnival these days you will
see the Face Painting Stall. Children (and adults too!)
enjoy having their faces painted, it adds to the
atmosphere of the occasion, and it can enhance the
theme by adding living colour to the proceedings.
So often, though, face painting is not thought out
properly. The painters may be issued with the wrong
materials that take too long to achieve a required
design, or the designs are too complicated, leaving a
long frustrated queue of disappointed children.

This book will help to change all that. Jean-Paul
Alègre and the Theatre du Fil d'Ariane have created
a series of exciting, dramatic designs that would
please any potential face painter. They are simple,
artistic and impressive. You do not need to be a
professional actor or artist to execute these designs,
a child could do them. On the following page I have
suggested suitable face paints that you might use,
with some general do's and don'ts. Anyone can
create these amazing designs for themselves. But
don't take my word for it, try them out for yourselves.

What make-up should be used? There are three basic
types of make-up. There are the simple crayons that
can be bought in any toy shop, there is the grease
paint used in most theatres, and then there are the
water based paints that will wash off easily with soap
and water. If you are face painting for large numbers
in public places I would recommend the water based
paints as the easiest to use. They can be applied quite
simply with a make-up sponge or a paint brush and
all you need beside your materials is a jar of water.

Jean-Paul Alègre and his company have used Leichner make-up for the designs in this book, they make both grease paints and water based paints so you can take your choice. I would also recommend Aquacolour paints by a company called Kryolan which make a wide range of colours and palates. If you have difficulty in obtaining any of these products locally it is possible to order them from a company called Theatre Zoo in Earlham Street, London, WC1, telephone number 01-836 3150.

Points to Remember For Face Painting

Organise your materials before you start.

Prepare your model. Make sure to pin back the hair so that you do not cover it with make-up.

Paint on your base first and then allow to dry before using any colour on top. This make-up only takes a few seconds to dry.

You can use your fingers to blend colours and create special effects.

Draw in lines carefully with a brush and then fill in the detail.

Keep it simple. That way you will keep the dramatic effect of these designs. If you add too much detail it will detract.

Allergies

You may be questioned about the suitability of these paints for people with allergic conditions. The manufacturers recommended in this book test their products very thoroughly before putting them on the market, so I feel you can safely reassure any worried model. Anyone with skin allergies must be careful how they remove the make-up. I would suggest that the water-based paints are the safest to use as they can be removed with soap and water. If grease paint is being used it might be advisable to keep a pot of non-allergic cleansing cream at hand in case of emergency.

The Bee

This make-up demands careful attention to detail and is designed to be seen in close up.

First circle the eyes with black as far as the hairline and descending down over the cheek bones. Fill it in with white and carefully draw in the lines with a fine brush. Fill in the rest of the base including the nose. Above the nose draw in the head and the antennae which you fill in with black. The secret of this make-up lies in the design of the mouth. Draw a white circle in the centre of the mouth encompassing the lips. Fill it in with white and draw a black circle round it leaving out the space below the nose. You will notice how this make up changes cleverly as the expressions change on the face.

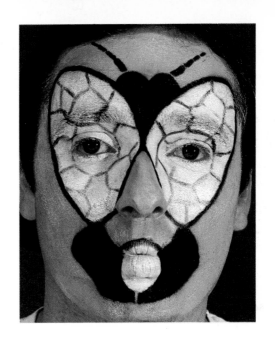

The Duckling

Draw in the black lines round the eyes and fill in
with white. Then draw in the large "clown eyes" and
fill those in with yellow. Take care not to smudge it
with the white. Draw in the beak above the mouth,
stretching it out over the cheeks. Fill it in with white,
and don't forget the little black dots on the nostrils.
Use a deep colour to surround the make-up to make
it stand out better.

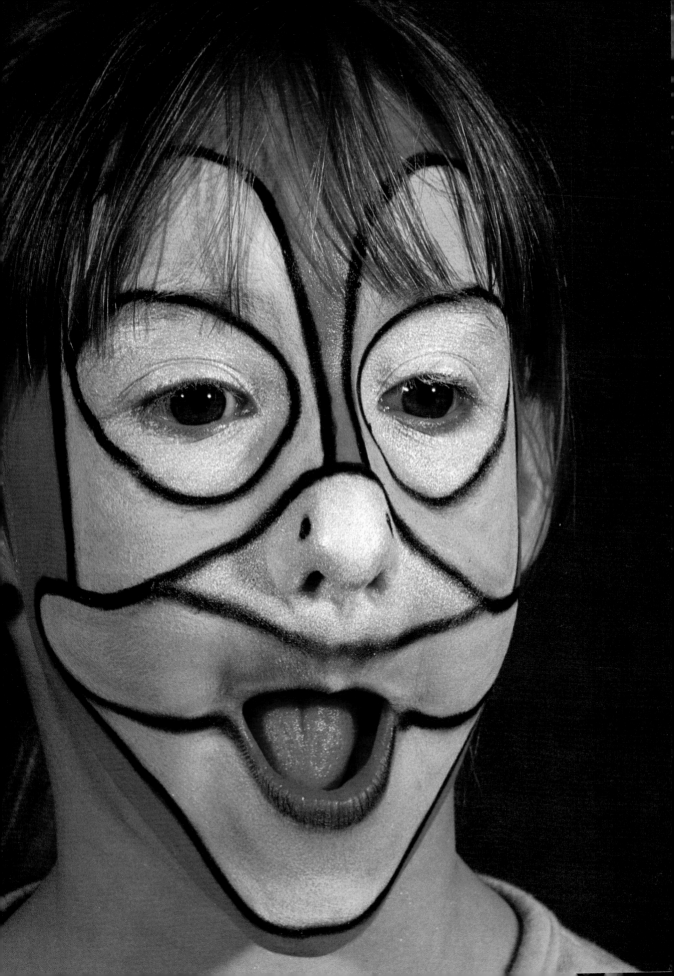

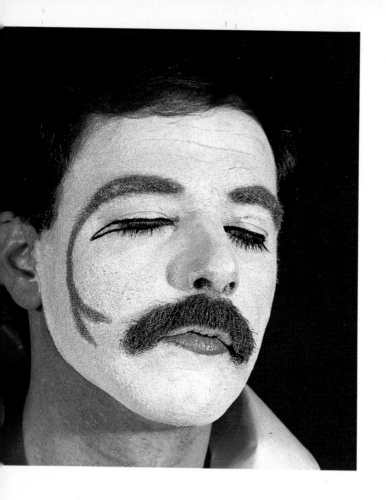

The Golden Magician

First fill in a white base. The eyebrows and moustache are then painted in with a gold pencil. This has to be grease paint as you then have to sprinkle it with gold dust. Be very careful not to get gold dust in the eyes. An original touch of this design is the elongation of one of the eyebrows. Paint the lips gold, and outline the eye with a thin black line.

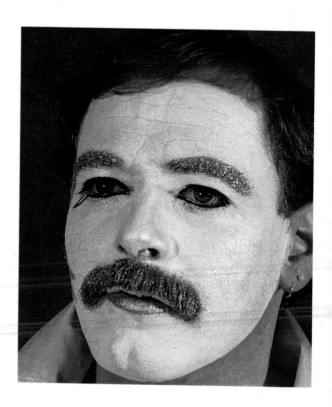

The Snake

This make-up lengthens the face. Paint on a thick white smooth base. Don't draw anything on the lower half of the face, just underline the lips in pink. From the end of the nose draw in the fine markings of the body of a serpent. Draw round the eyes in the same way. Draw in a fine line from the nostril up to the cheek and out above the cheekbone. Fill the part above the make-up with gold and green dots. Detail: Don't make up the upper lid in order to give a good effect when the lids are closed.

The Grey Cat

Use a grey make-up for this face which you can mix yourself using the black and white. Using a black line draw in a semi-circle below the lower lip without making the lip up. Cross the mouth with a vertical black line which will join up with the nose. Outline the eyes with white, and then carefully mix the white and grey areas. Finally draw in the black and grey markings all over the face.

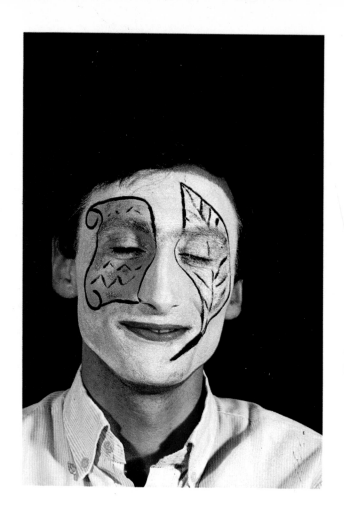

The Writer

This fantasy make-up is designed for close up rather than to be seen on stage. After covering the face with a white base, frame one of the eyes to represent a parchment. Draw a pen on the other eye taking care to surround the eyelids equally. Use some gold dust to add another dimension to this make-up if you are using grease paint.

The Storyteller

This make-up in contrast to the others is designed to have a dramatic effect from a distance. The lines are drawn in carefully to emphasise the features, and the colours used, particularly the gold and the silver are particularly effective from a distance.

The Sky

The whole face becomes the sky in this fantasy make-up. A thick blue base covers the face. The lips are white. One eye becomes a cloud and the other a sun. The eyes are joined by a rainbow. Some drops of rain on one cheek, some rays of sun on the other. Do not forget to outline the eyes in black so that the different expressions on the face can be noticed.

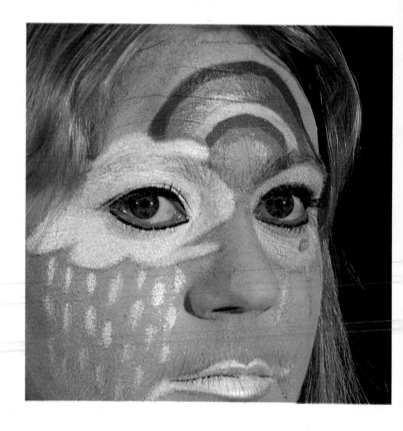

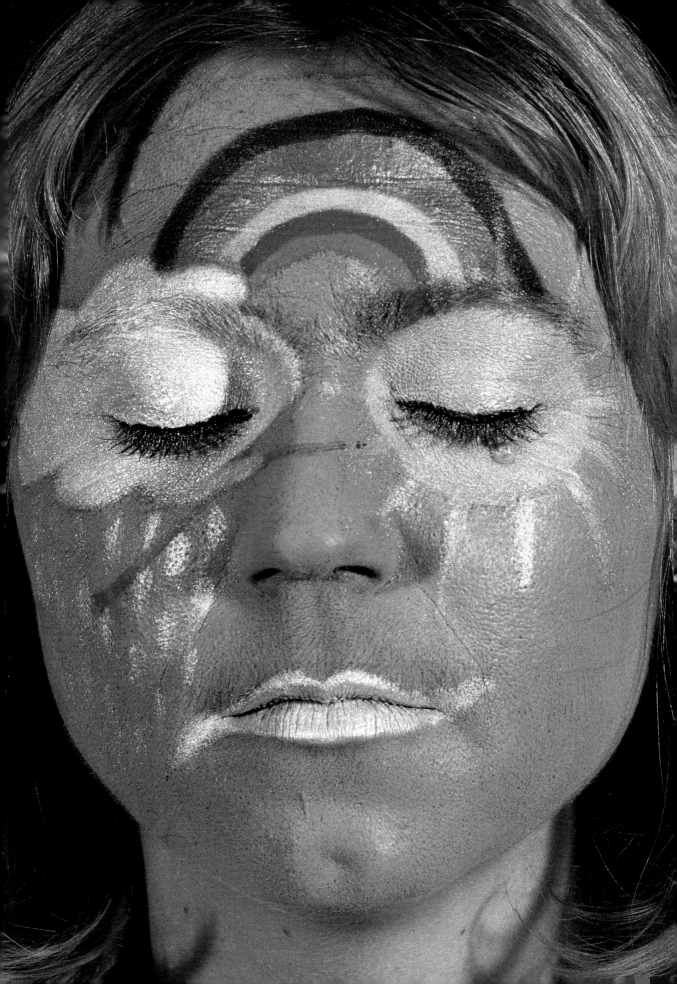

Leaves

On a smooth white base, draw two
large leaves to surround and
underline the eyes. Use black to
paint in the veins. Lightly colour
the lips and draw in a stem in
black down the centre of the
mouth.

The White Clown

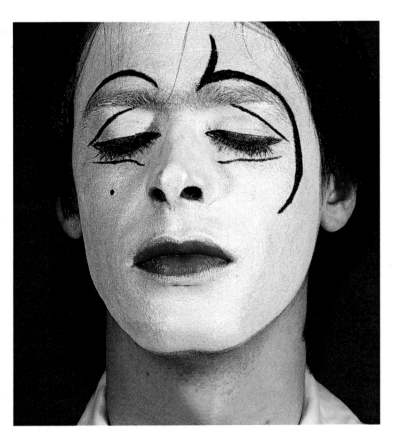

A simple but effective make-up when it is done clearly. A white base carefully extended to cover the face. The traditional eyebrows of the White Clown, one longer than the other. A very red mouth, and don't forget the black freckle on the cheek.

The White Rabbit

Paint on a white base, then draw in the lines around the eyes and the markings above the eyes. Paint in the moustache on either side of the nostrils, not forgetting the little black spots between the nose and the mouth. Don't underline the mouth merely cover it with the white base, but mark in the two little teeth and the red spot on the nose. You can highlight this make-up with a pink colour painted under the chin and on the neck.

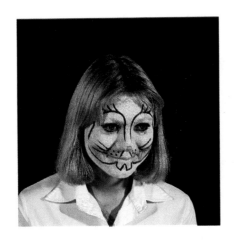

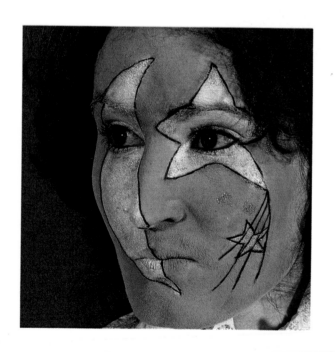

Night

Paint on a blue base but instead of having it all the same colour try and shade lighter and darker areas to make it stand out. Draw a crescent moon round one eye using part of the nose and the mouth. Draw in a star round the other eye and fill them both in with white.

The Seagull

First paint on the white base. Draw in the outline of the gull but take care not to surround the eye as it gives a better impression of movement in the wings if the eye is only partially covered. Make sure that you underline the eyes. Fill in your seagull with blue and then carefully paint in the shading with white.

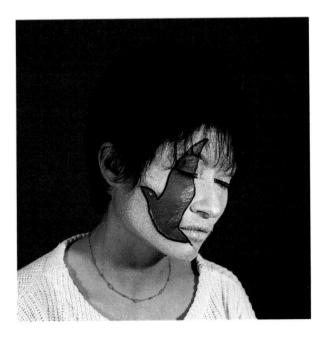

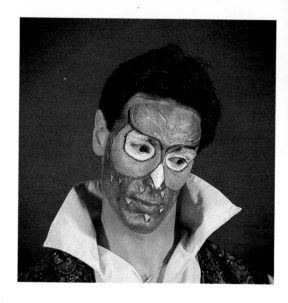

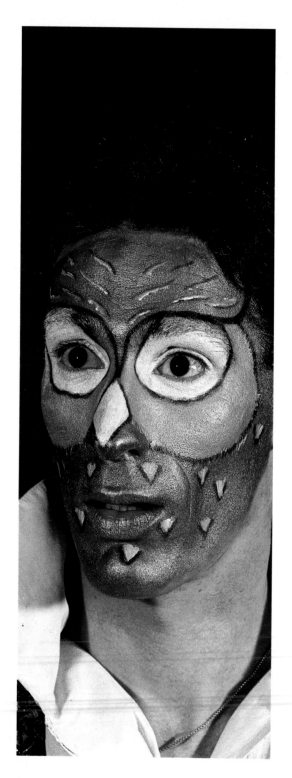

The Owl

This make-up is more complicated and takes longer than the others but is very effective when completed. First paint in the light and dark brown areas, allow them to dry and then draw in the eyes and the beak. Fill those in with white. Notice the way the nostrils are painted so that from a distance you get the impression of a beak. Break up the base with white triangles and with black and white streaks.

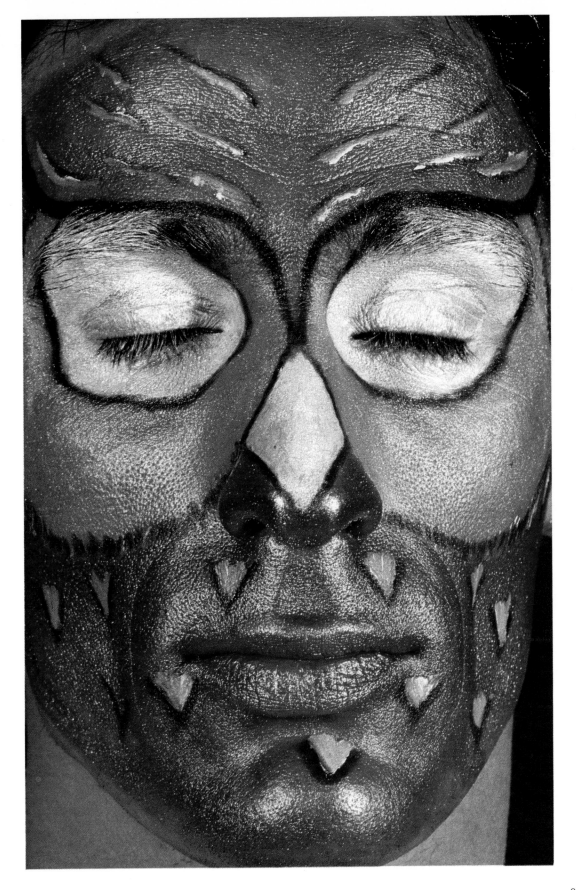

The Painter

A blue base for most of the face with the palette painted
in white. The palette is dotted with colours and note
how the green is used to disguise the nose. The paint
brush leans across the other part of the face and the lips
are gently underlined.

The Swan

A simple white base with only the eye and the eyebrow outlined. The eye of the model becomes the body of the swan. Use gentle colours for the swan and possibly some gold dust if you are using grease paint. Do not outline the lips.

The Bull

A dark grey base is painted over most of the
face with a lighter grey on the nose. The eyes
and mouth are white outlined in black so
that they stand out from the grey. The horns
are painted in black and the make-up is
lightened by a red circle on the forehead.

The Dog

Paint on a brown base. Outline the eyes with black, they are separated by the white on the nose. Notice the fine white lines above the eyebrows. The small nose is drawn in with black. The mouth is disguised by a vertical black line. Little whiskers and spots are drawn in above the top lip. The eyebrows are drawn very high on the forehead, and little white streaks are drawn in on the point of the chin.

The Leopard

Paint on a brown base and mark in the spots with fine lines. Paint the tip of the nose red, lower and flatten it to give the shape of the animal's nose. Paint in a triangle for the mouth. Fill in with white and draw in the whiskers and spots at the side of the mouth and nose.

The Bear

Paint a dark brown base and blacken the eyebrows. Large round circles round the eyes. From the centre of the nose paint a large white circle which stretches over the cheeks and ends on the cleft of the chin. Paint in a black spot at the end of the nose. Do not paint in the lips, but lighten the make-up with red on the cleft of the chin.

The Pink Cat

The pink cat is made by blending together a partly white and partly pink base, divided by fine white lines. The eyes are enlarged and well outlined. The mouth is divided by a black line with the little pink nose painted in at the tip of the model's nose. You will notice the wide variety of expressions that this make-up can give to the face.

Make-up lives!

On Stage!

Here are some photographs of actors from the Theatre du Fil
d'Ariane preparing their make-up.

Come on! Join us on a rare trip backstage.

On the Street!

In the classroom!

Follow us first into the dressing rooms of a Big Top where the actors are preparing for one of their shows. The atmosphere is tense.

In a dressing room the actors are getting ready. They are concentrating hard in spite of the cold.

Let us go into another dressing room.

For the more difficult stages they help each other, and gradually the face becomes a living palette of colour, a brilliant make-up carefully and painstakingly executed.

In contrast – look at the chaos on the dressing table!

Sometimes the make-up has to be less subtle and more exaggerated, especially if it is to be seen under strong lighting or from a great distance.

You can see two examples of this type of make-up on this page.

It is while the actor is alone with his mirror and his make-up in his dressing room, that he has the chance to look behind the colours on his face, and think deeply about the character he is about to play.

As you can see from these two photographs, one of which was taken during a rehearsal, make up does have an important part to play in creating a show.

Finishing touches with pencils and brushes!

The deserted dressing table – a chaos of make-up!

After our trip backstage let us go out among the public. There we can see the make-up live, smudge, crack up! There we can hear what people think. There we can see the contact between the artists and the children. It is rather like a party, but often a quiet calm party because they are communicating.

Unlike a mask, make-up does not hide the face. It's value is that it is a *living* mask that can change with the moods and expressions on the model's face.

'If only you always looked so sweet!'

'Why have you chosen a bird make-up?'
'I don't know . . . it gives me a feeling of freedom!'

'Mummy! I want a happy make-up!'
'You had better choose a princess!'

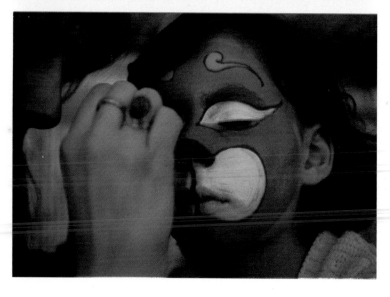

'Don't, rub it off! We are going to take a photo to send to your grandmother!'

'Alright it's fun! But what about your clothes!'

After the make-up sessions each child who has been made up is invited to take part in a short improvisation. The subject cannot be determined until the characters have been gathered together to see what combinations are available!

An example was when one actress had mostly animals – a cat, a tiger, a little wolf etc. etc. and then a cowboy! Out of the blue the little boy playing the wolf said, 'Now I'm going to eat the cowboy!'

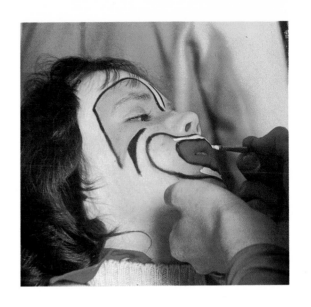

Finally, a series of photographs in black and white. By leaving out the colour you will be able to see more clearly how the markings are painted in.

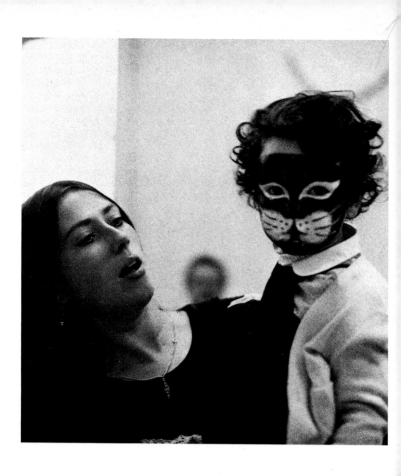

Look how alive these faces of the artists and the children are! The make-up seems to form a bond between them.

Now it is your turn!
Pick up your pencils,
brushes and palettes
and have a party!

Good Luck!

The Theatre du Fil d'Ariane

Based at Perreux-sur-Marne and at Vincennes in France, The Theatre du Fil d'Ariane employs a dozen actors-and-technicians who present plays for adults and children. They have also featured in several broadcasts on radio and television. Since 1986 it has been a regional company of the Ile-de-France. The following have been it's principal productions.

1970 **Poasis** – A creative collection of poetry and songs – La Perreux – Peronne.

1972 **Francois Le Betourne** – A creative collection by Francois Villon. – Le Perreux – Theatre du Val-du-Marne – Saint-Maur International Festival of Montrejeau – South West Theatre in the Round.

1973 **Waiting for Godot** by Samuel Beckett – Le Perreux – 4th Roger Vitrac Festival.

1974 **Adrien** – A creative collection – Auditorium of the Palais du Louvre as part of the Exhibition 'L'Enfant et les Images'.
Les Jouers d'Images – a theatrical blending of movement and make-up created at the Museum of Decorative Art. Later presented as part of the Animation du Haut Quercy, the Animation du Bassin du Longwy, The Salon de L'Enfance, September meetings at Senlis etc . . .

1975 **La Fete en Plein Air** by Vaclav Havel – Le Perreux Roger Vitrac's 5th Festival, – Cultural Centre of Toulouse – Festival of Orleans – Longwy.
Tutti Frutti, creative collection – Theatre du jardin d'Acclimation Paris – Animation du Haut Quercy – Longwy – Nancy – Rouen.

1976 **Soleil en Bouille** after Aristophane – Roger Vitrac's 6th Festival – Cahors – Brive – Marais Cultural Centre, Paris.
A series of broadcasts for TFI and FR3 (Early morning shows with Annick Beauchamps and Jean-Pierre Guerin)

1977 **Ecoute La Bruit de la Mer** by Jean-Paul Alègre – Marais Cultural Centre Paris.

1978   **Sidi Cine** by Georges Berreby – Theatre de L'Aire Libre,
        Montparnasse. This production was chosen to represent
        France at the 11th Festival at Sitges in Spain.
        The Theatre du Fil d'Ariane worked all winter at the
        Villages des Enfants of Annie Famose and Isabelle Mir
        at Avoriaz.

1979   **Maquillages de Fete** published by Editions Dessain
        et Tolra in French was awarded the diploma
        Loisirs-Jeunes, the prize Jeunes Annees, and the Label
        Recre A2. A series of broadcasts followed by Antenne 2
        with Dorothee and for TFI with Claude Pierrard.
        Festivals included Roubaix, Sens, Angouleme, Bordeaux,
        Bar-le-Duc, Lyon, Evreux, Vernon, Roanne, Niort,
        Verdun, Grenoble, Vierson, Bourges, Louviers.

1980   **La Fete en Plein Air** by Vaclav Havel was brought
        back in a new version for the opening of the new
        Cultural Centre of Perreux.

1981   **Colonel Cody dit Buffalo Bill** by Jean-Paul Alègre from
        Indians by Arthur Kopitt was created at the Cultural
        Centre of Bords-de-Marne. Because of its great success
        this production ran there until 1983, (with the group
        'Nuits de Theatre') and in Festivals at Bourges, Bordeaux,
        The Cultural Centre at Clamart, The Cultural Centre at
        Courrieres, Region Nord/Pas-de-Calais etc.

1982   Editions Dessain et Tolra published **Animation de Fete**
        the second book by the company.
        On tour with Buffalo Bill – took part in the broadcast
        with Eve Ruggieri of 'Nino Rota – Musique au Coeur'
        Toured with Cirque d'Hiver.

1983   Broadcast of Carneval de Recre A2 with Dorothee and
        Jacky. Took part in Musique au Coeur – Rossini –
        (Eve Ruggieri) **Maquillages de Fete** reached its sixth
        edition and was translated into English, German and
        Dutch.

1984   **Des Nuages et Quelques Sourires** by Jean-Paul Alègre
        was produced at the Cultural Centre at Bords-de-Marne.
        The company was chosen by S.P.O.N.T.E. to organise the
        first national make-up competition.

1985   **Ecoute la Bruit de la Mer** was reproduced in a new
        version under an enormous 4000 seater Big Top at
        Porte de Pantin. The production was co-produced by the
        C.L.D.C. (Centres de Loisirs et de Diffusion Culturelle)
        The production was then presented at the Cultural
        Centres at Bords-de-Marne and Courrieres, and on tour
        throughout France.

1986 **Des Nuages et Quelques Sourires**. The Theatre du
Fil d'Ariane became a Regional Company of the Ile de
France. The new production of 'Des Nuages et Quelques
Sourires' by Jean-Paul Alègre was performed by T.P.E.L.
of Lausanne. It played in Geneva and then went on tour
throughout France.

Encoute la Bruit de la Mer was produced by the Theatre
du Clin d'oeil at Verneuil-sur-Avre and the Atelier
theatre at Coutances, then by the Theatre d'Arlequin at
Cherbourg.

1987 Preparations for a grand production on Louis X1.
Tour of **Traviata** by Samuel Beckett.